POWHER
Play!

A WOMEN'S
EMPOWERMENT GUIDE

SHANTERA L. CHATMAN, MBA

PowHer Play

A WOMEN'S EMPOWERMENT GUIDE

Shantera L. Chatman, MBA

Pure Thoughts Publishing, LLC

This document is geared towards providing exact and reliable information in regards to the topic and issue covered. The publication is sold with the idea that the publisher is not required to render accounting, officially permitted, or otherwise, qualified services. If advice is necessary, legal or professional, a practiced individual in the profession should be ordered.

From a Declaration of Principles which was accepted and approved equally by a Committee of the American Bar Association and a Committee of Publishers and Associations.

In no way is it legal to reproduce, duplicate, or transmit any part of this document in either electronic means or in printed format. Recording of this publication is strictly prohibited and any storage of this document is not allowed unless with written permission from the publisher. All rights reserved.

The information provided herein is stated to be truthful and consistent, in that any liability, in terms of inattention or otherwise, by any usage or abuse of any policies, processes, or directions contained within is the solitary and utter responsibility of the recipient reader. Under no circumstances will any legal responsibility or blame be held against the publisher for any reparation, damages, or monetary loss due to the information herein, either directly or indirectly. Respective authors own all copyrights not held by the publisher.

PowHer Play

The information herein is offered for informational purposes solely, and is universal as so. The presentation of the information is without contract or any type of guarantee assurance.

The trademarks that are used are without any consent, and the publication of the trademark is without permission or backing by the trademark owner. All trademarks and brands within this book are for clarifying purposes only and are the owned by the owners themselves, not affiliated with this document.

ISBN: 978-1-943409-11-2

On a Personal Note...

When I was young, I used to like to assemble puzzles. It didn't matter if the puzzle was 50 pieces or 500. I just liked trying to figure out how to create the picture. As I have gotten older, I realize that life is a puzzle, and we try everyday to complete our own images. I am now aware that I live my life the same way that I would assemble a puzzle. I always find the edges first. Those are my boundaries. From there, I start to build the picture until it is finished. Like you, my puzzle is incomplete, and it will remain that way until I leave this earth, but the image I am creating is getting clearer every day.

I hope this book helps you to add pieces to your puzzle and to create an image you are proud of.

This book is dedicated to the one woman and three men whose images and voices have helped me to define mine.

To Mama, Eldrick, Tyrelle, and especially Pierre...

The woman I am today is a reflection of the love, support and patience you have shown me. Thank you for accepting me for who I am. I love you all.

PowHer Play

Table of Contents

1

Empowerment: A Definition

"The empowered woman is powerful beyond measure and beautiful beyond description."

-Steve Maraboli

Women's empowerment is a term that gets used a lot. It is used by speakers. It is used by authors everywhere, especially if they are trying to make a point that has to do with women's self-esteem, engagement in the workplace, or women in the community. More often than not, we use the words, but we rarely define them. Before we get started, I want to provide three definitions that I hope will help clarify what I mean when I say women's empowerment. Those three definitions are for empowerment, women's empowerment, and PowHer, which is part of the title of this book. It is my hope that these definitions will help you as we go through this journey together of defining women's empowerment for ourselves (Yes, I'm coming along for the ride with you).

The first word that we want to define is empowerment. Empowerment means that you have the power or authority to do something. Someone has given you, or *you* have given *yourself* the authority and/or permission to move forward on a particular task. That's pretty simple, right? Now, when we talk about women's empowerment, we're talking about involving women fully in any situation. In general, women's empowerment involves empowering women to participate completely in their life and endeavors, and also increasing the quality of their lives for their families and for their communities. Women's empowerment tends to be a little more all-encompassing, because now we're talking about ensuring that a woman has all of the tools she needs to move forward. It's important to note that women's empowerment affects not only a woman, but her family as well. I believe that once you empower a woman, you're actually empowering her community. The last term I want to discuss is PowHer. This is a term that I coined while working with my women's foundation. It means a woman's great ability to do or act upon anything that she desires. It's going one step further. It's not about society giving a woman permission to do something. It is *you*, giving *yourself* permission to act on your great abilities. We all have great abilities. Understand that you have the ability to move forward or travel down a path that you desire.

You may be asking yourself...

1. *What does all of this have to do with me?*
2. *Why do you think I need to know these definitions?*

That's Easy!

1. *You need to know this to help you move forward. Leo Martin Ganace said, "Keep moving forward. It's the way to live life."*
2. *You need to understand and define empowerment for yourself.*

I gave you Webster's definition of empowerment. How I interpret the definition and how you interpret it will be totally different.

Ask yourself, "What does this mean to me?" How do you choose to express your understanding of empowerment or your understanding of PowHer? I know it's not simple, because you can ask the question, but getting to the answer sometimes can be difficult because it's very personal. You have to ask yourself several questions.

Tough Questions About YOU:

1. *What am I giving myself permission to do?*
2. *What am I empowering myself to do?*
3. *When do I start?*

Notice, I didn't say who has *given* you permission to move forward. Why? Because you don't need anybody's permission to do anything. You should and can empower yourself. The point is, you are the only one who needs to understand your definition of empowerment. When you're trying to understand that definition, you will most likely have to ask yourself questions. One really tough question is:

Who Am I?

Defining who you are is probably one of the biggest tasks you'll ever have to accomplish, because it requires a tremendous amount of thought, and you have to be very intentional about understanding what you want. In order to discover who you are, and in order to get to the answer to that question, I'm going to provide you with a few more questions that you can ask yourself to get the ball rolling.

Who Am I List

1. *What am I passionate about?*
2. *What are some of the things that I absolutely love to do?*
3. *What are the most important things in my life?*
4. *What/Who makes me smile?*
5. *How do I describe "me" in 5 words or less?*

These are some pretty tough questions, and it may take some time to come up with some of the answers, but that's okay. Some of them may be pretty easy, but some of them you may need to think about, and that's okay. Take your time. Defining who you are and understanding who you are is not a race. You don't have to get it done today. You don't even have to get it done tomorrow, but you do have to commit to get it done.

It takes some people years to understand who they truly are, because we're all constantly evolving. We're changing. Some of the answers may be different tomorrow than they are today, and that's all right, as long as you're okay with the answers. Understanding who you are is worth the time, so put in the effort. Try your best to be truthful when you answer the questions. Once you have determined who you are and what your definition of empowerment means, there's only one thing that you need to do, and that's stand in it. Stand in your truth. Read the answers to the questions often. Know that the person you are is enough, and *you* can accomplish anything you put your mind to.

     I remember when I started my career as a consultant at Johnson Space Center. The great thing about consulting is that you get to move around and work in different industries. It was a great time to understand space flight, to understand what goes into building a space shuttle. That was great, but what I wasn't prepared for was to see women in a way that I had not been exposed to. I was working in a male-dominated field with very few women. I noticed that most women I met were very intentional about being "less than". By that, I mean acting inferior to their male counterparts. For example, there was a young lady who decided to quit her job after only working for six months. This was her first job out of college, and she decided to quit because she was being harassed. Rather than speak up for herself, she decided that it wasn't worth it. I thought, "So you decided you are not worth it." For the life of me, I just couldn't understand it. I didn't understand why she would ruin what could potentially have been a great career, and just walk away without trying to right the wrong that had been done to her. Don't get me wrong, I understand that harassment is hard to prove, and she was young, but what seemed to strike a nerve with me was that it wasn't a one-off situation. Once I heard about the first one, more cases kept occurring over the next several months. There were so many examples of women who decided not to speak up, who decided not to be empowered, who felt like it was better just to move along in order to get along.

I will say that this was one of the biggest reasons I decided to start a foundation for women. It wasn't because I felt like I had a lot to give and I was so strong. I did, however, understand that women did not need to be objectified, and there was a voice that didn't seem to be heard. I felt like I could at least provide an opportunity and a space for women to be able to move forward in a better way and be more comfortable. It's the one thing that embodies empowerment. I created a space where true PowHer is fostered and can grow organically. I'm incredibly proud of what my PowHer has allowed me to do.

<u>PowHer Point</u>

Ensure that you understand your definition of women's empowerment and where you fit in it. Understand that it's different for everyone. My definition of empowerment is going to be different from yours, and how I interpret it for myself is going to be different from the next woman's interpretation. Different definitions mean different overall perspectives. Trust that you have developed the best definition for you, and not for your mom or your best friend. Living someone else's definition of women's empowerment can lead to unhappy and unhealthy relationships.

PowHer Play

PowHer Planning

_____

_____

_____

_____

_____

_____

_____

_____

_____

_____

_____

_____

_____

_____

_____

Assertion vs. Aggression

"Be who you are and say how you feel, because those who mind don't matter and those who matter don't mind."

-Dr. Seuss

To be assertive is perceived as being self-assured. To be aggressive is perceived as being on the offense. Notice how those two words evoke different feelings. Assertiveness gives a feeling of strength; an image of someone standing up for what they believe in. Aggression tends to promote a feeling of tension. Imagine a person standing up for what they believe in, but using an elevated voice and inappropriate language to get their point across. Women's empowerment is about knowing the difference between the two. In any given situation, ask yourself:

1. *Which do I personify on a daily basis?*
2. *How am I perceived at work?*
3. *How am I perceived at home?*
4. *In highly stressful situations, how do I react?*
5. *Looking back on previous discussions, am I happy with how I have behaved?*

The one thing that I've learned about aggressiveness and assertiveness is that there are perceptions that go along with each. There will be positive and negative perceptions about who you are, and the person you are trying to be. Sometimes those perceptions are right, and sometimes they're wrong. Sometime your actions will be completely misinterpreted, and those perceptions are not as positive. The key to being an empowered woman is owning your actions (and the perceptions that come along with them), both good and bad. The bottom line is that it's not about what you are trying to say, it's how you are received.

Remember, in any communication, there are two roles: the sender and the receiver. The receiver is the most important.

If you were received inappropriately, that means you need to work harder to convey your message. Owning your message and the perceptions that come along with it is the first part. Deciding how you want to move forward is the next. Always remember that you have to take corrective action. If for some reason you appeared to be overly aggressive in a situation, whether at work or at home, you have to figure out how you're going to fix it. The whole point of communication is to get your point across to someone else.

Acknowledging your behaviors and owning them is a big step. The second step is to be intentional about how you behave. The third step is to be unapologetic. Those are the keys to women's empowerment. Think about it, when you speak in front of an audience, or even to friends and family, you want to be sure that you are representing your true values. You have to be intentional about the person you want to be and how you represent her. Don't get me wrong, there will be times when the situation will call for a bit of aggression. Only you will know when that time comes - time to speak up a little louder, time to stand up. Understand that it's perfectly fine to be aggressive, as long as you understand what the consequences of those actions are going to be. Understand that your actions may not be perceived as positive. In life, we have to understand that each interaction is not always going to have a positive outcome.

Not everyone is going to be happy with how you speak or how you present yourself. Women's empowerment is about being flexible enough to understand that there are going to be several versions of you. There will be the assertive you, who steps out into the world to speak out about a topic that you are passionate about. There will also be the aggressive you, who may appear when someone is trying to attack your family, your friends, or even yourself.

Most of the time, you will be trying to make a point. You will be trying to build a case that you hope will come out in your favor.

So, how does it work?

Consider this situation. You schedule a meeting with your boss to discuss a possible raise. What do you think your main goal should be in this situation? To get the raise, right? In this case, I would advise you to plan to be assertive. The one part of your plan that you can't predict is this: You don't know what they will say. You can't predict if they're going to be offended by one of your points, or even just by your walking in room, but what you should know is that you are going to be strong enough to continue the conversation, even if you have to be a little aggressive. Understand that whether you need to be assertive or aggressive depends on your audience. A simple task like stepping up and saying, "Hi. My name is Claire Johnson," and firmly shaking the hand of someone across from you can be perceived negatively. There's a chance they're going to think negatively about your strong appearance. They're going to think that you've got no business walking up to them like you own the place. In my opinion, that's their issue to deal with. You are being the best you that you can be.

I remember when I first started working with women. I was volunteering at a women's shelter. I was still working as a consultant, but at night I would go to a women's shelter once a week and teach what they called 'assertiveness classes'. In these classes, we did a little of everything. We talked about building careers, handshakes, eye contact, and even the strength in our voices. We talked about the difference between aggression and assertion, because as you can imagine, those at a women's shelter had been displaced from various situations, from drug abuse to abusive relationships at home, but there was a lot of anger. There was a lot of resentment, and we had to figure out how to get past that. In order to get past the resentment and anger, you have to work through the aggression. What I learned from those women is that even if bad things happen, and you're so angry that you find yourself in a situation that you don't feel like you can overcome, there are always baby steps that you can take. Baby steps are small steps that allow you to make progress and celebrate your success.

The process of moving forward or getting over a bad situation is very, very difficult. The point is to keep moving forward, whether it is making eye contact with a man for the first time in years, or even shaking hands with a stranger without breaking down and crying. Those are baby steps. For the ladies in the shelter, the main goal was to keep moving forward. I loved teaching that class, because we saw women change overnight. I saw ladies go from being homeless to building careers, and growing their families in a positive way. I was able to see them change and I felt like I had a part in that change. It was in the assertiveness class, that I learned a valuable lesson as well. Being assertive is not about making someone understand your point of view. It's about knowing your presence alone garners respect. It is up to you to demand that respect, not just from your colleagues, family, and friends, but also from yourself.

PowHer Point

Choose positivity. By that, I mean choose the positive road for you. Sometimes aggression comes from a negative place, and there is a better way or a better action that can be taken to get your point across. Take the time to figure out the positive actions and words necessary to get what you want. It's worth the time.

PowHer Play

PowHer Planning

_____

_____

_____

_____

_____

_____

_____

_____

_____

_____

_____

_____

_____

_____

_____

_____

3

Decision Making

"Decisions are the hardest thing to make, especially when it is a choice between where you should be and where you want to be."

-Author Unknown

Women sometime get a bad reputation for being indecisive. It's not a good reputation to have. To know that people feel like women can't make decisions on their own, or that men feel like they have to make decisions for women, doesn't make us feel proud. Feeling empowered to make a decision based on what you want or need is a true sign of strength, and in some cases, a sign of courage. Most of the time, we make our decisions based on how it makes others feel. What I want to challenge you to do is to make decisions based on how or what you feel. You may be thinking that it's easy for me to say this. You're maybe saying, *"Hey, you don't have my family. You don't have my friends. You don't have my boss. Who are you to say I should make decisions based on how I feel?"* You're right. I don't. I don't have your family, but I have my own. I have my own friends. The one thing I have learned is this: I'm never going to be able to please them anyway. Regardless of the situation, someone's always going to be unhappy.

There's always someone who's going to feel like you made the wrong choice. In that case, why not be happy with yourself? Why not make the decision that pleases you? Work will always be there. It may not be in the same company. It may not be with the same people, but there will always be work for you to do. Sometimes, you may need to shake things up a bit and step out of your "pleasing everybody" box. Trust me, I am the worst at it. I'm a people pleaser. Understanding that in order to move forward you have to step out of that box is a stretch, but a lot of times, it's a necessary stretch. True friends will always love you, even if you make decisions that don't please them. The same goes with family. I know that it can seem difficult to make a decision when your family doesn't believe it's the right decision, or when your friends don't believe it's the right decision, and you may get a little apprehensive about making them mad at you. You know what? Sometimes it's okay for them to be mad at you, because friends and family should be there, even if you make the wrong decision or if you don't make the decision they feel like you should. Unfortunately, it doesn't always work out that way. If you make a decision that some disagree with, they may decide they no longer want to be with you. Do want to know what I say to that? *Oh well! It's their loss.*

In those unfortunate situations, I pray that you have the strength to stand strong in your conviction. I hope you continue to move forward in your decision, not back-pedal, and know that by choosing you, you are always making the right decision. Find the strength inside to just move forward. Those people (friends or family) that are supposed to be there, will be. Those that are not most likely have not been there for a while (you just haven't paid attention).

I remember a situation at work where I heard someone say something that shook me. In my opinion, it expressed a racial bias that I knew was going to make it very difficult for me to move forward working with that person. As luck would have it, that person was my boss.

Imagine being in a career that you really like, and all of a sudden, someone says something that changes everything. In a second, everything was different, and I knew it. I knew I needed to say something. The bias that was being discussed was inappropriate, and it had changed the way I felt about the company completely. What I didn't realize would happen to me was the turmoil inside, the internal fight that I had with myself as to whether or not I should even speak up. I decided to speak up and talk to someone I felt was a mentor. I wasn't prepared for what was going to happen next. I wasn't prepared for that person to tell me to just let it go. I wasn't prepared for that person to say, *"Oh, you must have heard them wrong. No. That doesn't sound like her at all. You should have just talked about it. I'm sure it's not what you think."* I wasn't prepared for the whole thing to turn on me, and to essentially be told to be quiet about it. For weeks, I didn't say anything. I was internally beating myself up for not speaking up, and also emotionally breaking down. After a long conversation with myself, I realized that it wasn't about them. It wasn't about who was going to be angry with me. I decided to speak up. I decided to confront my boss and do the one thing that a lot of people are afraid to do, and that's report the incident to human resources. Once it was reported, people started to talk, and then things got bad. People were angry. I saw my leaders turn their backs on me. No one spoke to me for months. I was terribly disappointed that the people I assumed were good people were being so mean. I was exhausted from dealing with all of the emotion. After a while, I turned a corner, because I knew that I was making the right decision for me.

All of a sudden, what used to make me cry every day no longer affected me. I smiled a lot. I was not smiling about the situation in general, or smiling about what was said to me. I was smiling because it was no longer stressful. I'd done what I knew needed to be done, and I was standing in what I believed to be my truth. That made all the difference. Those so-called leaders were still angry (some of them probably still are angry) but it didn't matter to me, because I was no longer angry. I was no longer sad, and that's what's important.

PowHer Point

The Voice

There is a voice inside of you

That whispers all day long,

"I feel that this is right for me,

I know that this is wrong."

No teacher, preacher, parent, friend

Or wise man can decide

What's right for you-just listen to

To voice that speaks inside

-Author Unknown

PowHer Play

PowHer Planning

4

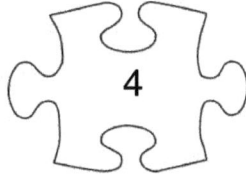

Negotiations

"Let us never negotiate out of fear. But let us never fear to negotiate."

-JFK

Negotiation is something that a lot of women tend to struggle with. Women also struggle with asking for what they want, and furthermore, with standing their ground. Statistics show that women don't negotiate for what they want, or at the very least, ask for what they want.

Empowerment is about standing in your truth and being YOU. PowHer is about understanding your worth. Both have a lot to do with why it's so important to negotiate. I was doing some reading recently and found some statistics that were astounding. The title of the article I read was "Women Don't Negotiate". Let me ask you something...

Did you know???

* *Women say they feel apprehensive about negotiations 2X more than men.*
* *Men initiate negotiations of any kind 4X more than women do.*
* *Women will pay as much as $1300 more on the price of a car to avoid negotiating. WOW!*

NOTE: *This is a conscious decision that women are making to pay more for a car rather than discuss the price.*

* *20% of adult women, about 22 million people, say they will never negotiate.*

So, what happens when we don't negotiate? We suffer. We lose our voice and are subject to what others think we should have or pay.

Men are four times more likely to negotiate their salary, which means that by the age of sixty, they will have earned a half a million dollars more than a woman. Women who do negotiate earn about a million dollars more than women who decide not to negotiate. That's a lot of money. That's a lot of income that we are losing just by not saying, "No. I feel like I deserve a little bit more" or "How about if I ask you for this much rather than that?" We've all heard the saying, "It doesn't hurt to ask." For some of us, it does hurt. It is a space that women, in general, are not as comfortable with. So, my question to you is this:

What is negotiation, and what are we really trying to accomplish?

It's really just a tool. Negotiation is a tool to change the status quo, to change what other people are thinking. The major goal is to share your point of view about the situation. If it's a salary you are negotiating, you're sharing what you feel you deserve. It's up to that other person to tell you why they are only willing to pay a certain amount. Another goal is to listen. You are there to hear the other person out, just as you hope that they're there to hear you out. The bottom line here is that you're trying to come to a reasonable solution. They give a little, you give a little, and before you know it, you have a resolution in place.

What does this have to do with women's empowerment?

Honestly, it has a lot to do with women's empowerment. It's about knowing your worth and not selling yourself short. Do not settle for anything less than you feel you deserve. I'm still working on this myself. I am very intentional when it comes to negotiations. I rehearse a lot. Negotiating makes me uncomfortable, but I have to do it. Life is about stretching beyond your personal limits, and for me it's a huge stretch. For you, it may not be, but if it is, there are a few things that we can do to make ourselves better at negotiations. Don't wait for others to negotiate for you, do not assume that your spouse is going to negotiate the price of your car, and do not assume that your boss is going to come to you with a salary increase that you feel is appropriate.

Think about it, the person on the other side of the table, the car salesman, he's looking to ensure that he has a great commission. Your boss wants to make sure he/she is not spending too much money for the company. You are there to take care of you. They're there to take care of their own best interests. Take control of your own life. Be in the driver's seat. It does you no good to stay in the passenger seat of your career and allow someone else to steer you in a direction that you don't want to go. Know your value and do not be afraid to ask for it.

So, how do you negotiate? How do you get better at negotiating?

Well, you know what they say: *Practice makes perfect*. You can practice at home with your friends and family. I don't like doing dishes. I love to cook, but I hate washing dishes, so I negotiated with my husband. "I will cook meals every night (or most nights), but if you want me to cook every night, you're going to have to do the dishes," I said. He came back to me with his offer. Instead of doing the dishes every night, he proposed we use paper plates. That was a great idea, and not a bad negotiation rehearsal. It was simple and painless. We are talking about simple conversations. If you feel you need practice, start with something painless. Try negotiating the time you arrive at work with your boss. If that goes well, try an extra half hour for lunch.

These are simple conversations that you can have to get comfortable with negotiation. Before you know it, you'll be ready to have a big conversation about negotiating your salary, or even to negotiate the price of a car. When I think about negotiation, I think about my husband Pierre. I call him the Master Negotiator. He used to be in sales and he enjoys the conversations. He enjoys haggling back and forth on the prices of cars and homes. You may know someone who loves to negotiate too.

I remember when Pierre and I were looking for our first home. We'd been in our neighborhood of choice looking at homes for weeks. We'd set our sights on a townhouse. I really loved it. I thought it was a nice place for us to start our lives as a married couple. We were in negotiations over the price, and I watched my husband be very strong as he stated what he wanted to pay for the property. He stood his ground and was very aggressive when he needed to be, but he was mostly assertive. We were down to what I thought were pennies on the dollar. We were negotiating over fifty dollars. My husband was standing on a price for what he felt we should pay for the townhouse, and the sellers were fifty dollars off. My husband refused to budge. I was losing my mind, because I was thinking, "Oh my gosh. We're going to lose our house over fifty dollars." I remember screaming at my husband and telling him, "I have fifty-dollars in my purse. I will give you the fifty bucks if you let us have this house. Please don't lose this house for us." Long story short, after a day or two more of negotiations, we decided not to get the house. My husband would not cave in, and I was devastated. I could not understand. It was just fifty bucks. He told me, "Honestly, I don't think we should move any further. I don't feel like we should pay more. If we keep giving, they're going to keep taking." Even though I was angry because I wanted the house, I understood. When you continue to give, even if it's fifty dollars, someone will take and take until you have nothing left. There were so many other things on the table that we had to negotiate besides the price that we were not going to come out of the situation feeling good about it. As it turned out, about a week or two later, we bought a much bigger house for much less. At that point, I realized that had I kept pushing the fifty dollars and convinced my husband to take the house, we would have missed out on a better deal. In that moment, I learned to be patient.

I had to let it come to me and to understand that I didn't lose a house over fifty dollars. Instead, I gained a bigger home for several thousand less. What I learned from that situation and what I continue to learn from my husband is that you have to stand up for what you believe is your worth, and don't move from it. Once you get to that point, you have to be strong enough to know that if people walk away from you, it's going to be for your betterment.

PowHer Point

The essence of women's empowerment is knowing who you are and what your worth is, and not wavering from that knowledge. Stand strong and say, "No. I'm not going to move, because I know my value." It's empowering to stand in your truth and not let anyone move you. Make it a goal to always stand strong in who you are and what you want, and surround yourself with those who respect you for it.

PowHer Planning

_____

_____

_____

_____

_____

_____

_____

_____

_____

_____

_____

_____

_____

_____

Your Voice

"A woman with a voice is by definition a strong woman. But the search to find that voice can be remarkably difficult."
-Melinda Gates

Your voice is who you are. In the first chapter, we defined empowerment and PowHer. As you define those words for yourself, you are also defining your voice. Knowing your voice and what it means to be you is a true sign of PowHer. It's your true sense of strength. It's your ability to understand and act on your voice, not anyone else's. That's your calling card. Sometimes your voice is what makes you unique and sometimes your voice is what draws people to you. I'm not talking about your actual voice, how you sound when you speak, but instead what you stand for. For instance, I pride myself on standing up for diversity. I'm an advocate for the inclusion of women and other underrepresented groups in the workplace.

I've been working with women for almost ten years now. My voice is very clear to me. It has made me recognizable in my community. It's who I am. It's my truth. Now you have to ask yourself, *"What is my truth?"*

A few questions for you to consider…

1. *What are you willing to stand up for?*
2. *What are you willing to speak on if needed?*
3. *What does that voice sound like?*
4. *What do you refuse to be silenced about?*

Let me caution you, once you find your truth and decide what you are willing to stand up for, that's when you're going to find those who want to silence you the most.

During this time is when your opposition will come forward, and your voice will have to be stronger than ever.

Those that don't believe in what you stand for are going to try to silence you. For those people, your job is going to be simple:

DO NOT LET THEM

Once you allow someone to take your voice away, they're basically taking you away. No one likes to be opposed. We don't want to be the person who's always challenged, so what do we try to do? We try to stop the challengers. I have it on good authority that it's healthy to embrace resistance. Meet challenges head-on. When you do, you'll find that it makes you stronger. If you're strong in your convictions and you know your voice, you're not going to allow anyone to silence you. You're not going to allow them to put you in the corner. Remember what Patrick Swayze said: "No one puts Baby in the corner." That's not what being empowered is about. It's not what showing your PowHer is. Women's empowerment is about understanding that voice, and knowing that you cannot be silenced. You are not a trinket to be put on a shelf. You are a person with strength and power, and you are not afraid to show it.

There are times, of course, when your voice needs to be heard in different ways. It could be through your actions, because we speak sometimes without saying a word. Our actions speak louder than our words and therefore, we have different ways of showing and representing our voices. Sometimes it's through writing. This book is a reflection of my voice. This book is telling people outside of my community how I feel about my love for women, for our growth, for empowerment and the process of being empowered. Your voice may give speeches all over the world. Your voice may be a singing voice. It may be a poet or it may just take action. It may show up in a situation where someone says that you shouldn't show up. It may show up when you decide to speak about something that others don't feel like you should be. The example I gave about racial bias and the biases as they were communicated to me at work is an example of me letting my voice be heard.

Pierre was talking to me about that situation one night. I was crying about what I should do, and whether or not I should speak up. My husband said something to me that I hadn't heard him say before. He said, "This is your duty. You have the responsibility to say something about that." He said, "It is not because you are working at this company. It's your duty because you founded an organization that preaches every day to women to speak up, to have a voice, to let their voice be heard, and to step out of their comfort zone. The Chatman Women's Foundation is you, and you have a responsibility to everyone that has ever supported you, but more importantly, you have a

responsibility to yourself to speak up and speak out."
When he said that to me, it lit a fire. I still was a little
apprehensive, but at the same time, I knew what I needed
to do. I knew how I needed to do it, and I moved forward.
I began taking steps to allow my voice to be heard in a way
that I'd never allowed it to be heard before. I said things
that I never really thought I'd have to say, and I found the
strength in myself that I didn't know I had. Sometimes,
someone else reminds you who you are and how they've
interpreted your voice, and that becomes your strength to
move forward.

<u>PowHer Point</u>

Your voice is who you are. Don't let anyone take it away from you, no matter the circumstances. Sometimes people will try to silence you, put words in your mouth, or twist your words. Don't allow it to happen. It may be difficult and it may be uncomfortable, but understand that your voice is worth it. Those who listen to your voice and depend on its truth will thank you.

PowHer Planning

_____

_____

_____

_____

_____

_____

_____

_____

_____

_____

_____

_____

_____

_____

6

The MRS Degree

"Never lose yourself in a relationship. Love your partner fiercely, but always follow your own unique dreams and desires. Be true to you."
-Author Unknown

PowHer Play

The MRS Degree. It's described as going to college to find your husband. It is, in my opinion, the total opposite of women's empowerment, and the total opposite of PowHer. It's relying on someone else, and PowHer is about independence. PowHer is about standing on your own and making decisions that reflect who you are as a person.

I'm not saying that young women should not meet their mates in college. It happens everyday. I take issue with the intention. Some go to college specifically to find a man. I've come to realize that MRS degrees still exist. This thought process happens more often than I initially thought. I thought that getting a MRS degree was something from back in the day, but I was wrong. Let me be clear, there is nothing wrong with looking for love, just not a lease. You should not consider going to an institution of higher learning just to find someone to take care of you. That is definitely not PowHer, and it shouldn't be any woman's intent.

The MRS degree is not a joke. The MRS degree is offensive. It's offensive to women who are trying to do better for themselves. It's offensive to women who are building families on their own, and to those who are trying to get an education. I know several women who would kill for the opportunity to get an education and it has nothing to do with a man. Education shouldn't be taken for granted. I didn't understand what was meant by a MRS degree until I attended a women's group meeting and everyone was introducing themselves one at a time. I remember saying, "Hi, I'm Shantera. I'm the founder of the Chatman Women's Foundation. I graduated in 1998 from Texas A&M University and I graduated with a degree in Information and Operations Management." Everyone's introductions were very similar, until we made it to one woman. She introduced herself very differently. She shared her name and her school, but after she gave us what degree she graduated with and her age, she went on to say, "Even though I got a degree in journalism, I really went to school just to get my MRS degree. She held up her ring finger and she showed us this huge diamond on her finger and she said, "Because I received my MRS degree, I don't have to work. I get to stay home every day and have babies." WOW! Everyone went silent. I don't think anyone knew how to respond. How do you respond to someone whose aspiration was to just find a man? In this day and age, it was really shocking to hear. She was actually very young. All I could think in my head is, "She's selling herself short." I'm not saying that she doesn't have a wonderful husband, nor am I saying that staying at home and having children is not honorable. Being a mom is one of the most difficult things to do, as well as one of the most honorable. She was not bragging about being a mom, she was bragging about being kept. I felt like there was more to her story, but I decided not to pursue understanding it at that moment. I did, however, find that there were several other women who had the same testimony. It's disheartening to know that we are selling ourselves so short by assuming that we need someone else in order to be successful, or that we're not willing to put in the work ourselves to be successful.

PowHer Point

Don't sell yourself short. You're more than a wife and a mother. If you want more, go for it. Don't take the easy road to life. Your family is looking to you to set the example. You don't need anyone to validate your greatness. Your greatness comes from within, not from a ring.

PowHer Play

PowHer Planning

_____

_____

_____

_____

_____

_____

_____

_____

_____

_____

_____

_____

_____

Who Am I?

"Don't get confused between what people say you are and who you know you are."
-Oprah

Everywhere we go, there is someone trying to tell us what's best for us. What we should do, what's the best way to speak, and what we should and should not eat. It makes it really difficult to understand who we are when everyone is trying to make decisions for us. Whether it is the television, family, or friends, everyone's giving you their opinions on the best way of being. Determining who you are means that you understand what you want and don't want out of life. One of the first things you can do is take inventory.

Think about some of the things you've always wanted, or wanted to be. Did you want to be an astronaut when you were little? Did you want to have kids? Now that you have your list, what are the things on the list that you no longer want? Ask yourself,

"Why don't I want those things anymore?"

Is it because someone told you not to want those things? Is it because someone said it was too hard and you decided that it wasn't worth the effort?

The moral here is to make sure your decisions are yours and not anyone else's. A lot of times, we allow others to get inside of our heads. There are so many people that are whispering in our ears about what they think we should do. Before long, we lose ourselves in trying to please other people. The big questions we should be asking ourselves are:

How do I know if I've lost my voice?

How do I know who I am?

How do I know my truth?

How do I know?

It's a feeling. You feel comfort. Don't do something out of obligation for someone else. A lot of people have tried to tell me I need to have kids. "You should have children", they say. I never felt that it was my time, so I didn't allow anyone to influence my decisions about my body or my family. No one else can do that for you. You may want to get input from your spouse or your friends, but the ultimate decision maker is *YOU*. No one can tell you what you aspire to. I strongly believe in writing down your goals. If they are written down, you can read them daily and put steps in place to achieve them. Of course, just because you're writing them down it doesn't mean that they are going to happen in that exact way, but at least you have a plan.

I remember when my brother was a little boy, he used to ask the simplest questions. He always wanted to know who was in charge. He would ask, "Who's the boss of me?" He really wanted to try to understand who he should listen to in any situation. I was over twenty years old when he was young, and he felt like he had too many people telling him what to do. He needed clarification. You should ask yourself that question a lot.

Who is the boss of me?

Hopefully, you hear back a resounding answer.

<u>YOU</u>. You are the boss of YOU.

You give yourself permission to go to work every day. You gave yourself permission to buy those new shoes. You gave yourself permission to get married or to raise a family. You decide, not anyone else, because you're not a baby anymore. You don't need five different people telling you want to do. You don't need someone to hold your hand to cross the street. You can make your own decisions.

PowHer Point

There is a great quote that says, "A woman should be two things, who and what she wants." To me, that is everything. Think about it. Let that resonate and decide for yourself who you want to be and what you want to be. After you decide, take action to reach your goals. It really is that simple.

PowHer Play

PowHer Planning

_____

_____

_____

_____

_____

_____

_____

_____

_____

_____

_____

_____

_____

8

Women Helping Women

"As you grow older, you will discover that you have two hands, one for helping yourself, the other for helping others."
-Audrey Hepburn

Madeleine Albright has a quote that says "There is a special place in hell for women who don't help other women." I'm not sure about the hell part, but I surely believe that women should help other women. Why? Well, why not? Should we fight one another and try to bury each other? Should we pull each other down while we try to climb the corporate ladder? That doesn't make any sense to me. Why not help someone to do better? You never know, the person you help climb the ladder may turn around one day and help you get where you want to be.

I always say, "The money is not coming out of my pocket." To help someone get promoted is not going to stop my paycheck or make my paycheck any smaller. As a matter of fact, I think that once we help someone, we get back two or three times more, because we get that positivity turned back on ourselves. It may not be from the person that we help, but just in general.

Women of color have the reputation of not working well together at all. Why is this? The naysayers say we have too much attitude. We're too opinionated. In actuality, we can work together. I work with women a lot and if there is an issue, it has nothing to do with gender or race. Several of my business ventures have been with women, and they have absolutely no issues at all. Of course, there are times when we disagree, but in business, that's what happens. We disagree. In life, that's what we do, but strong empowered women are mature enough to understand that one disappointment doesn't mean the business is over. It doesn't mean that the friendship is over. Having PowHer means that you understand that someone else can have a strong point of view and not only should you listen to that opinion, but you should respect it. In actuality, it doesn't have anything to do with race. It doesn't have anything to do with anything. We're just people.

Reality TV would have us believe that we're conniving and willing to stab our friends in the back just to get a good man. That's simply not true, and, we're not living in a reality TV show. The reality that we see on TV is not reality. It is made up. It is made up of acting and a lot of motionless motion. For us PowHerful women, it has created extra work. We are left with the job of educating young women about the "real" way women should act and interact with one another. It's extremely important for women to mentor other woman. That's one of the reasons why I created PowHer Play. PowHer Play is an event that's hosted by my foundation in Houston, Texas. It's a breakfast for professional women to mentor one another. Women come together for breakfast, and they talk about their careers and the challenges that they've had climbing the ladder. The conversations are very candid. No one is trying to hurt anyone. Everyone is trying to help. We all share our experiences in hopes that they help others. What I've been most proud of with PowHer Play is the continued conversations that happen after the event is over. I'm extremely proud of women feeling like they have other women that they can count on, that they can network with, and that they can help build their businesses with. To me, that's what women's empowerment means. It means helping others, and PowHer means being secure in yourself to help other women move ahead, knowing that it doesn't make you in any way inferior or beneath them. We need to start to unlearn the behaviors that we see on TV and that we hear on the news. It's time to unlearn the selfishness and learn how to help, to learn humility, and to learn selflessness.

It may be a little bit harder for society as a whole to get to that point, but for us as women, I don't feel like we're going to be able to succeed without getting past the negativity. If we don't unlearn the negativity soon, we will find ourselves in a male-dominated world where we feel like our voices are no longer being heard. Working in corporate America, I've run into what I've called the Omarosa syndrome. Omarosa is a strong businesswoman that appeared on the TV show The Apprentice. The image Omarosa portrayed affected me professionally. I found myself defending black women and correcting stereotypes based on what my colleagues saw on TV. I deemed it the Omarosa syndrome, because everyone seemed to use that as the mark for how black women behave. I did not want to be associated with an image that was not positive and that I did not create. Unfortunately, the show was a hit, and her image remained the dominant image for black women. That image from years ago, all the way to the image that we see now on television, help to set a standard for how women are perceived, as well as how women treat each other. It's not entertainment to watch women be a sideshow. It's not fun to assume that all black women fight, are loud, have attitudes, and use our bodies to build our careers.

We should understand that it's our responsibility to pull each other up and to create an image of women that is stronger, better, and more powerful than it has been in years. We have more women in leadership positions than ever before. I feel like that's completely lost on some of the younger generation, and we need to ensure that we are doing our part to set a better example for our young women when it comes to helping others. We should build on the positive imagery and help the younger generation see women for who we are... strong, talented, and beautiful.

PowHer Point

You have nothing to lose and so much to gain by helping others. What's for you is for you, period. Helping someone else is not going to take away from what you are meant to have in any way. I recently saw a quote on social media that said, "Girls compete with one another. Women empower each other." That couldn't be any truer, because immaturity says that you have to compete. Once you're mature, strong, and empowered, you know that it's your responsibility to empower others.

PowHer Planning

_____

_____

_____

_____

_____

_____

_____

_____

_____

_____

_____

_____

_____

_____

The Gift of Service

"You have not lived today until you have done something for someone who can never repay you."
-John Bunyun

PowHer Play

We're each put here to give something. There is something in each one of us that is considered a gift, whether it's our singing voice, our writing, our ability to love, to build families, to develop youth, or to educate, but we're all here for a specific reason. As we go through this journey of putting together the pieces of the puzzle of who we are, we find and understand what that reason is. We each have our God-given gifts that we need to share with the world. In order to receive more, you need to be open to giving more. We've talked about women helping other women and being able to share openly and mentor women. That is giving. When we take part in activities that help another person, we are giving the most precious gift of all… our time. We do ourselves a disservice when we decide not to give back. I think about the "pay it forward" trend that's happening right now. I hear stories of people purchasing a cup of coffee for the person standing in line behind them, or even paying lay-away accounts in the department store. You may ask yourself, "Why are they doing these things? What do they expect in return?" Not everyone gives in order to receive something in return. Some people give because it makes them feel good about themselves.

For me, serving women and sharing what I've learned is my gift to the world. Your gift to the world may be something totally different. Your gift may be to sing or to write beautiful poetry. If you have a gift (tangible or intangible) that you are willing to give simply to bring a smile to someone's face, please share it. Do not let anyone tell you otherwise.

Question: **What have you given or what have you been given by someone else that has changed your life?**

Think about that for a minute. Who has given you something that you didn't expect? Who's opened the door for you for a new job? Who's provided you with a down payment on a new car that you didn't expect? I can guarantee you there's at least one instance where you've been given something that you didn't feel like you deserved. Once you realize what that is, be willing to pay it forward to someone else. Give to someone that may not feel like they deserve anything as well.

When I decided to start the Chatman Women's Foundation, I was bombarded with questions. People would say, "You don't have to do this. Why are you giving back to these people? These are strangers. You're a professional woman. You're in corporate America. Just let the company write a check. Why are you doing this?" My favorite question was from a stranger who said to me, "Who do you think you are to start something like this?" My answer to that young woman was pretty simple: "I'm Shantera Chatman and I'm doing this because I want to." That was it. I didn't feel like I needed to give her any more of an explanation than that. Even today when I get that question, I give a similar answer. I'm helping women. I'm building up women in my community because I feel like I should. I've been called to do it. I've been lucky enough to have family and friends around me that have allowed me to grow and thrive and constantly strive to be a better person. I want to be that for somebody else. I want to be able to help other women move forward. It is my hope and it is my prayer that I'm doing that, even with this book right now. I hope that I'm inspiring you to do more and helping you to decide what gift you're willing to give.

PowHer Point

"I give, not because I have to, but because I know what it feels like to have nothing."

I've given financially to women because I know what that feels like not to have money and I want to help someone else. Quite frankly, you don't need a reason to help. Your reason could be 'just because', and that's a good enough reason for me.

PowHer Play

PowHer Planning

_____

_____

_____

_____

_____

_____

_____

_____

_____

_____

_____

_____

_____

_____

_____

_____

_____

10

The Empty Cup

"I have come to believe that caring for myself is not self indulgent. Caring for myself is an act of survival."
-Audre Lorde

PowHer Play

I have to admit, I suffer from a disease. It's called "trying-to-be-everything-to-everyone-itis". I recognize it, and at times it causes me to stretch myself really thin. "You can't pour from an empty cup. Take care of yourself first" When I first read this quote, it resonated so deeply with me. I've tried for years to take care of everyone else and be what everyone wanted me to be, with no regard for myself. What do I need to be for my husband? What do I need to be for my mom? What do I need to be for my family? Recently, it's become harder to be all things to all people. I've learned the hard way that I can't continue to operate by putting everyone else first.

I implore you to learn from my mistake and put yourself first. Choose you. Before you spend your last ounce of strength helping someone else, choose to focus on you, your health, your body, and your sanity. Think of it like this: You're on an airplane, and before you take off the flight attendant gives you instructions for survival. "In case of decreased air pressure, put your oxygen mask on first before trying to help someone else." What are they saying? Save your life first. You're no good to anyone else until you've taken care of yourself. Giving yourself oxygen, time to breathe, and time to replenish will help so many people in ways that you cannot imagine. When you're fully functional and healthy, you make better decisions. When you decide to choose you, you are a better person for everyone around you. I've learned that there is a true healing power in the staycation. The staycation is when you just stay at home and unplug. You don't have to spend a ton of money to go somewhere exotic and lay on the beach drinking a tropical drink. It's very difficult to unplug, I'll admit, with iPhones, iPads, Androids, Galaxy Pads, and many other electronic gadgets. Have you ever said, "I'm going to turn off my phone, not check emails, and just going to be here in my space?" If not, you should try it. By taking the time to relax, you're allowing you brain to rest. Don't worry about emails or social media. Use that time to focus on you.

There have been times when I've been so stressed out from work that my body has decided to shut down. I'd find myself with the flu, and because I was so tired, I couldn't get well. One time my husband said, "I think you need to take some time off. You haven't taken any time off work. You're constantly working. It's time to rest." I've been married long enough to know that if my husband suggests I do something, I take that suggestion very seriously. More often than not, it means that he's seen something in me that may be unhealthy. So I decided to take two weeks off. During those two weeks, I didn't do much of anything. I didn't check emails. Actually, I gave myself one day out of those two weeks to check email. I wasn't on the phone all the time, and there was not a lot of texting. I just stayed home. I watched TV when I wanted to watch TV. I listened to music when I wanted to listen to music, and I cooked when I wanted to cook. I allowed my body to rest, but also I allowed my brain to rest. After those two weeks, I was more productive. I went to work and I was able to make better decisions. I was clearer in my thoughts. I felt like I was able to listen at home when I needed to listen. I was able to take care of others a lot better than before.

Take a self-inventory. Sit for a minute and ask yourself a few questions.

1. *When was the last time you took a vacation with just you?*
2. *When was the last time you went for a long drive and didn't have the radio on, didn't talk on the telephone and just were left alone in your private thoughts?*
3. *When was the last time you didn't say a word, you just sat still and you just allowed yourself to have peace?*

If the answer is more than thirty days ago, take some time for you and realize that you can't pour anything into anyone if your cup is empty. You can do so much more with a full cup. The only way that you can refill your cup is to replenish and to reward yourself for all of your hard work.

PowHer Point

The problem with always putting others first is you've taught them that you come second. Think about it.

PowHer Planning

_____

_____

_____

_____

_____

_____

_____

_____

_____

_____

_____

_____

_____

_____

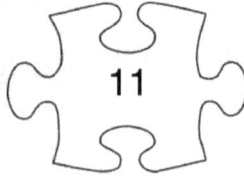

11

Speak Life

"Everyday as my day begins I give LIFE to my Faith, for I choose to Speak Life. I don't just BELIEVE... I Declare It as I Speak Favor and VICTORY!"
-MzGloria

When you look in the mirror, what do you see? When you look at yourself in the mirror, do you say anything? If you do say something, is it positive? Are you looking at yourself and saying, "Man. I need to be smaller. My hips are way too big"? Are you speaking life to yourself? When I say life, I mean positivity. Are you speaking strength? Are you speaking health? Are you telling yourself that you're great? If you're not, make a resolution to do so. Resolve to tell yourself that you're great, you're worthy, you are powerful, and you have the power to do anything that you want to do.

Understand that what we see on TV does not dictate who we are. What we say to ourselves is far more important than anything anyone else could say to us. Think about it, when you speak to yourself, you're speaking what will turn into your truth. I'm sure you have known people who are constantly saying, "I can't. I can't do this, I can't do that." After a while, guess what? They really can't. They really can't move forward without feeling pain. They really can't get the next promotion. They really can't, because they've talked themselves out of it. They've talked themselves out of whatever it is they kept saying they cannot do.

I try my best not to use the word can't, because it is probably one of the most dream-killing words that we can use. In place of can't, you should say 'I can' or 'I am'. Tell yourself what you are instead of what you are not, and don't wait for others to tell you what you can do. Of course, it's great to have affirmations every once in a while from others. It's great to get awards at work, or to feel appreciated by your family and friends, but what happens if they don't reward you? What happens if they don't recognize your hard work? Then you're left feeling like you didn't accomplish anything.

What would happen if you gave yourself kudos every time you did something great? What would happen if you looked at yourself in the mirror and said, "You are wonderful. You are doing great things today." What would happen if after you finished that project, you told yourself "Good job" or took yourself out to dinner? What would happen? Do you know what would happen? I know what would happen. You would be happy with yourself. You would not wait for someone else to affirm you. You would not need someone else to say something to make you feel good.

I was watching TV one day, and there was a really horrific story being presented. It was about a football player who had done some really bad things to his wife. As I watched the story, I saw some really terrible pictures of this woman's body, beaten and bruised. All of a sudden, I started to find myself getting really, really sad. I found myself upset, not because of what this guy had done, even though that was horrific. I was upset because of the story that was being told. They were presenting the story as though the guy didn't really do anything. There may have been things happening with the woman that we didn't know about, and she may have provoked her abuser. That was what made me sad, because I interpreted the story as saying that women have to understand the violence that happens to us, and to protect his career, she should have been quiet. That made me really angry. I felt like there was a soundtrack that was being played for this one particular woman, but also for other women who were watching. The message was, 'you have to deal with it'. We're going to take care of our own, because he's a million-dollar football player and women should figure out a way to deal with it privately. I started to think about what we as women would have to say to ourselves to get that soundtrack out of our heads. To get that soundtrack out of our heads, we would have to tell ourselves that we are not punching bags. We are not all of the things we are called by disrespectful men (and other women). We are worth him losing millions of dollars because, NEWSFLASH: ***Women are worth more than a football contract.***

When I saw that story of a NFL player beating and abusing his wife, it was like he was diminishing her worth. I imagined what she would have to do to get her worth back, to build herself back up, to increase her value. I imagined her, or anyone that finds herself in the same situation, saying, "No. I am better than this. I am worth more. I am strong. I am better off without him." We have to speak life over ourselves, even when others are saying something different.

PowHer Point

"The revolution will be live." – *Gil Scott-Heron*

Our struggle, what we are trying to accomplish as women has nothing to do with what is being played on television. It has everything to do with the soundtrack that's being played in our head. We must speak life over ourselves as it's not the responsibility of others to do so.

PowHer Planning

_____

_____

_____

_____

_____

_____

_____

_____

_____

_____

_____

_____

_____

_____

12

Embrace your <u>PowHer</u>

"It's NOW time to reclaim your POWER, you have always had it."
-Shelly Sullivan

PowHer Play

I read somewhere that creativity is intelligence having fun. We are all intelligent people. We all have our space where we are most comfortable. Allowing yourself and your intelligence to have fun and to see where it takes you is a freedom that is allowed to you by women's empowerment.

Being empowered means that you are allowing yourself to be free. PowHer is what we've been talking about all along. We've been talking about not underestimating ourselves, the strength that it takes to stand in our truth. What we are made of, what makes us strong, what makes us powerful. Each of these things are components of PowHer, and are different for each one of us. Each person reading this book is going to have a different way of interpreting the chapters, and will implement lessons learned very differently. Try to exhibit and embrace all of those gifts that you know you have inside of you, and build upon those gifts. Allow those gifts to show up and to have fun within your brain in order to bring forth a new revolution, so to speak, for women.

In football, a power play is an aggressive play where a lot of offensive players cover and move forward to block and create a clear path for a ballplayer. Someone is running down the field, and we are trying to clear the field to get our player to the end zone. PowHer Play is when women come together to help move each other forward and propel each one of us ahead. This book is your PowHer Play. Use it to help others and guide your network down a path of success. Use it to block anything and anyone that's standing in your way. Use the knowledge and the thoughts that you've conjured as you've read the chapters to build others up. Create a network that will be a force to surround you and to help you reach your goals.

PowHer Play

When I was volunteering at the women's shelter, I facilitated an assertiveness class. Halfway through class one day, a woman arrived late. I could tell right away that something was wrong. I saw that she'd been crying. She was still upset and I could see that her face was a little swollen. I thought, "Oh my goodness! She must have just come from an argument with her spouse or her husband or something." She looked battered. She sat in a corner and listened to us as we talked through our topic for the day. Everyone else in the room started to feel tense. You could see tears still running down her face. You could feel the fear in her. All of a sudden, her phone rang. She picked up the phone, and I think she accidentally pushed the speaker button, because everyone in the room heard her husband on the other end of the line. He was yelling the most hateful words to her. He was telling her that he was going to kill her and how she would never see her children again. It was horrible. I was heartbroken. You could see the devastation on her face. She was completely beaten down. It was an emotional beat down. It wasn't just on her face, but he was constantly beating her with his words as well. Then, I looked around the room and it wasn't just her. The entire room was in tears. Every woman in the room had tears coming from her eyes. Before I knew it, I'd lost control of the class. This was no longer an assertiveness class. It had become a help session. It was a counseling session that I felt ill prepared to handle. I rushed out to get help, and one of the other counselors from the shelter removed the woman from the class. In the meantime, I went back to trying to work with the ladies in the class. Another thirty minutes or so went by, and the class was over. Shortly after class, I was gathering my things and my thoughts at the same time. An older woman walked into the shelter conference room. She'd started to cry. I asked her if there was anything that I could do for her. She started to explain that she'd just received a call from the shelter saying that her daughter had been abused by her husband.

I soon realized that she was the mother of the woman from my class. The mom looked at me and she says, "How do you help someone that doesn't seem to want to be helped?" I just stared silently at her, because I didn't have an answer. She said, "The only thing I feel like I can do is to get custody of my grandkids, because this man is going to kill my daughter." It was in that moment that I realized that she felt helpless. She felt like even at the shelter, there were not enough people to protect her daughter. She wasn't big enough to protect her daughter, and no one at the shelter was going to be able to help.

PowHer and PowHer Play in general is about building something that's strong enough to help women move forward. In the situation at the shelter, the mother didn't feel like she could move forward, that there was nothing that she could do. With the knowledge that we have come together to gain, my hope is that you can help someone to move forward in a way that they didn't feel like they could. I hope that you are able to build a network that helps someone to acheive a goal that they didn't ever feel like they would be able to. You may not be able to block for everyone all of the time, but a few steps are better than none. Also, don't forget that while you are blocking for others, you should also block for yourself.

PowHer Point

PowHer- A woman's great ability to do or act upon anything that she desires.

It's not that society is giving women permission to do something. It is YOU, as a woman, giving *yourself* permission and acting on your great abilities. We all have them. Ladies, it's time to act.

About The Author

Shantera Chatman founded the Annual Women's Empowerment Conference in 2008 after volunteering for over a year at a local women's shelter. Before she knew it, the conference had become a movement that provided women with resources to enhance every aspect of their lives. Once Shantera realized how strong the empowerment message was to women in the community, she took steps to carry the message of empowerment beyond the conference.

She later formed the Chatman Women's Foundation that provides financial support to women building businesses, furthering their education, and even to those that need financial support to move into a new home from a shelter or other crisis institution. It is a reflection of not just Shantera's beliefs, but also the beliefs of the women living, growing, and thriving in and around the Houston community. With such a sturdy foundation and a strong following, the Foundation will be helping women for many years to come.

Shantera and her business partner own C+A Global Group, LLC, a boutique consultancy that focuses on strategic organizational engagement & adoption for Fortune 1000 companies. She frequently facilitates discussions on leadership, diversity and self-esteem at her alma mater, Texas A&M University. She has worked throughout her career to help others discover their leadership talents through group facilitation, motivational speeches and other workshops/seminars. Shantera has made it her mission to see women showcased in a different light in the workplace and at home. Often criticized for being "too smart", Shantera refuses to "dummy down" her message of power and self-worth. Her message of being true to oneself is genuine and clear. She stresses an unapologetic belief in self and strong values that will build a foundation that is unbreakable.

For more information about Shantera and The Chatman Women's Foundation, visit **chatmanwomensfoundation.org**.

www.PureThoughtsPublishingLLC.com

Pure Thoughts Publishing, LLC

www.ingramcontent.com/pod-product-compliance
Lightning Source LLC
Chambersburg PA
CBHW071624040426
42452CB00009B/1472